RING
THE DOORBELL
WITH YOUR
ELBOW

RING THE DOORBELL WITH YOUR ELBOW

A COOKBOOK OF "PORTABLES"

WILMA M. McCARTNEY

THE NEW ENGLAND PRESS
SHELBURNE, VERMONT

© 1981 by The New England Press, Inc.
Revised Edition
Previous edition © 1972 by Wilma M. McCartney

For additional copies write to:
The New England Press, Inc.
P.O. Box 525
Shelburne, Vermont 05482

Library of Congress Catalog Card Number: 80-84349
ISBN: 0-933050-07-0

Second Printing: September 1982
Third Printing: November 1983
Fourth Printing: June 1987

PRINTED IN THE UNITED STATES OF AMERICA

dedicated
with love to
"gammy"
an old doorbell ringer
with an expert elbow

PREFACE TO THE FIRST EDITION

"Ring the doorbell with your elbow" was a family expression when I was a child. It meant that you were invited to a party and that you would have to ring the bell with your elbow because your hands would be otherwise occupied carrying your contribution to the groaning board.

This collection of recipes has grown during the almost thirty years of my homemaking, party-going, and marriage to an Innkeeper. Credits for individual recipes are almost impossible, for many have come from newspapers, magazines, old files, assorted cookbooks, friends, and trial and error. Many are my own, developed by the patience and digestive juices of my family and friends. Many have incorporated the use of convenience foods, a trend of the times. All are portable.

When I take something to a party and do not anticipate being asked into the kitchen or muscling my way in, I attach a slip to the container giving heating or chilling directions; and, I make sure that the container I have brought, if I want it back, has my name taped on the underside.

The desserts served at the Shelburne Inn are my particular contribution to the Inn. I take a great deal of pride in producing them and am highly flattered that so many people have requested the recipes. That is one of the reasons for this little book.

All of the recipes that follow can be prepared ahead of time. Many of them freeze well.

I have tried <u>not</u> to include "old standards." Be adventuresome and try something new! Happy Ringing!

Wilma M. McCartney 1972

preface
to the
second edition

    This revised and enlarged edition of RING THE DOORBELL WITH YOUR ELBOW has been published because so many requests have come for the first edition which is now out of print. Needless to say, I was very pleased by the success of the first edition. To the old favorites in this book, I have added many new and exciting recipes which I hope you will enjoy. Finally, I wish to take this opportunity to thank all those who took the time to write me and share their suggestions and comments.

Wilma M. McCartney 1980

CONTENTS

hot hors d'oeuvres

annie's
asparagus canapés

25 slices thin, soft bread
8 ounces cream cheese
3 ounces bleu cheese
1 egg
1 package frozen asparagus spears
1 cup margarine or butter, melted.

Mix cream cheese, bleu cheese, and egg until smooth. Cook asparagus spears as directed on package. Drain well and cool. Trim crusts from bread. Roll each slice with rolling pin and put damp towel over slices to keep them from drying out. Spread each slice with cheese mixture and place an asparagus spear on each. Roll up tightly. Dip each roll in melted butter. Freeze on cookie sheet. When frozen, cut each roll into 3 pieces. Store in plastic bag in freezer. Makes 75 pieces. To serve: Put desired number of rolls on cookie sheet. Bake at 375° F. for about 10 minutes or until browned.

CURRIED MEAT TURNOVERS

FILLING

8 ounces cream cheese
½ cup butter
1½ cups flour
¼ teaspoon salt

Combine cream cheese and butter (both at room temperature) with flour and salt until well blended. Knead into ball and chill at least 1 hour. Roll out and cut into 3-inch rounds. Place a heaping teaspoon of cooled filling in center of each round. Fold over and crimp. Bake turnovers at 400° F. for 10-15 minutes.

¼ pound mushrooms, finely chopped
¼ pound ground beef, lamb, or fowl
1 tablespoon sherry
1 tablespoon soy sauce
¼ teaspoon sugar
1 teaspoon curry powder
½ teaspoon salt
1½ teaspoons cornstarch
2 tablespoons butter
1 cup chopped onions

In a skillet gently cook mushrooms and onions until transparent, not allowing butter to brown. Add all remaining ingredients and mix well. Cool.

☆ These turnovers may be made ahead and frozen. If you freeze them, defrost them for 1 hour before warming. Warm on cookie sheet in 400° F. oven for 3 minutes.

This is a great way to use up leftover meat. If you use freshly ground meat, cook filling longer.

LOBSTER ROLLS

½ cup butter
½ pound processed pasteurized cheese
1 pound lobster meat, fresh or frozen, cut finely
2 loaves very fresh sliced white bread

Melt butter and cheese together in a double boiler. Add lobster meat. Remove crusts from bread. Roll each slice very thin with rolling pin. Spread lobster mixture on bread. Roll up firmly and freeze. When ready to serve, cut each roll in half and brush with a little additional melted butter. Defrost and bake at 400° F. for 10-15 minutes. Be careful not to brown lobster rolls too much.

MINIATURE QUICHES

PASTRY

2 cups flour
1 teaspoon salt
3/4 cup soft butter
1/2 cup ice water

FILLING

8 slices bacon, crisp and
   crumbled
Grated Parmesan cheese
2 eggs
2 egg yolks
1 teaspoon dry mustard
1/2 teaspoon salt
Cayenne pepper
1/4 cup bacon fat
1/4 cup grated Parmesan cheese
2 1/4 cups light cream, warmed

Sift flour and salt together and cut in butter with a pastry blender. Work in ice water. Knead and roll out 1/4-inch thick on floured pastry cloth. Cut in 1 3/4-inch rounds and fit into miniature muffin pans. Makes 60.

Divide bacon into muffin tin rounds. Add a pinch of Parmesan to each. Mix together eggs, egg yolks, mustard, salt, cayenne pepper, bacon fat, and 1/4 cup Parmesan cheese. Add warmed cream. Blend well. Fill tarts with custard. Bake in preheated 425°F. oven for 5 minutes. Reduce heat to 325°F. and bake for additional 12 minutes or until puffed and brown. These may be frozen before baking and stored, covered. To serve, thaw and cook as above.

stuffed
mushroom
caps

35 medium mushrooms
1 cup butter, divided
1 large onion, finely chopped
½ package prepared stuffing
   mix
1 cup chicken bouillon
Salt and pepper to taste
Garlic salt to taste

Clean and remove stems from mushrooms. Chop stems and sauté with onions in ½ cup butter. Add stuffing mix, bouillon, salt, pepper, and garlic salt. Stuff caps with mixture. In a 10 x 15-inch pan melt the remaining ½ cup butter. Place mushrooms in pan. Bake at 350°F. for 10 minutes. Cool. Cover pan with foil. Freeze. To serve, bake unthawed and covered at 350°F. for 15 minutes. Remove foil and broil for 3-5 minutes.

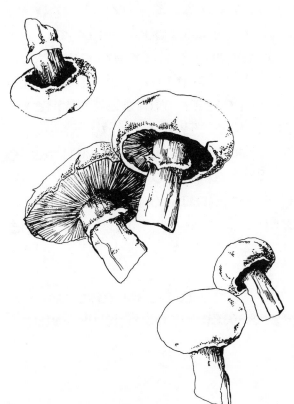

hot mushroom canapés

1 pound fresh mushrooms
Milk
4½ tablespoons butter, divided
2½ tablespoons flour
1 tablespoon grated onion

½ teaspoon curry powder
1 teaspoon Worcestershire
   sauce
Salt and pepper
Sherry (optional)

40 small toast squares

Put mushrooms (stems and caps) through food chopper or food processor, using steel blade, and save juice. Drain chopped mushrooms. To the juice add enough milk to measure 1 cup. Melt 2½ tablespoons butter in saucepan. Whisk in flour. Add juice and milk, stirring and cooking until smooth. Add onion, curry powder, Worcestershire sauce, and salt and pepper to taste. In a small skillet sauté mushrooms in 2 tablespoons of butter until tender. Add to sauce. Add a bit of sherry to taste. Cool. Spread on toast squares. Place on greased baking sheets. Bake in 400° F. oven until well heated or run under the broiler and watch carefully.

☆You can carry these ready-to-go to a party and bake them there. The filling freezes well if you don't want to use it all at once.

8

siamese canapés

½ cup creamy peanut butter
¼ cup mayonnaise
1 tablespoon lemon juice
1 teaspoon curry powder
1 clove garlic, crushed
1 cup chopped, cooked shrimp
½ cup chopped, golden raisins
¼ cup grated apple
¼ cup chopped onion
¼ cup chopped parsley
50 toast squares, crisp
(crusts off)

In a large bowl beat peanut butter and mayonnaise until creamy. Blend in other seasonings. Add the remaining ingredients. Refrigerate until ready to use. To serve, pile on toast squares and broil about 6 inches from heat until golden (about 3 minutes) or bake in hot oven (425°F.) until lightly brown, about 10 -12 minutes

chafing dish
MEATBALLS
& FRANKS

2 pounds ground round
1 slightly beaten egg
1 large onion, grated
Salt and pepper to taste
1 12 ounce bottle chili sauce
1 cup grape jelly
Juice of a lemon
2 pounds frankfurters, sliced
   diagonally 1/2 inch thick

Combine ground round, egg, onion, salt, and pepper. Mix and shape into 50-60 small balls. Combine chili sauce, jelly, and lemon juice. Drop meatballs into sauce and simmer until brown. Add franks. Cool and freeze. To serve, defrost and reheat slowly. Serve with picks.

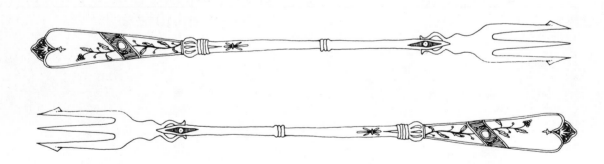

cold hors d'oeuvres

antipasto

½ cup olive oil

3 medium onions, chopped

½ cup vinegar

1 (12 ounce) bottle chili sauce

1 (14 ounce) bottle catsup

2 (6½-7 ounce) cans tuna fish

4 ounces sliced stuffed olives

1 (7¼ ounce) jar sweet pickled onions, halved

1 (8 ounce) jar mixed sweet pickles

Sauté onions in olive oil. Add vinegar, chili sauce, and catsup and bring to a boil. Remove from heat. In a separate bowl mix flaked tuna fish (drain if you use water pack) with its oil if you wish, and remaining ingredients. Combine both mixtures and refrigerate. This mixture keeps very well.

You may wish to add other things too, such as small chunks of salami, black olives, or button mushrooms.
☆ Serve with crackers.

CHEESE LOG

¼ pound sharp Cheddar cheese
3 ounces softened cream
   Cheese
¼ pound Roquefort cheese
2 tablespoons onion juice
1 teaspoon mayonnaise
¼ teaspoon Tabasco sauce
Paprika

Grate Cheddar cheese. Mix thoroughly with cream cheese and Roquefort. Add onion juice, mayonnaise, and Tabasco and mix well. Form mixture into a roll, or rolls, 1 inch in diameter. Roll on waxed paper that is covered with paprika. Wrap in freezer paper and freeze. To serve, defrost, slice, and serve with rye rounds or crackers.

TURKEY pâté

2 cups cooked, chopped turkey

2 tablespoons thinly sliced scallions

⅓ cup toasted ground almonds

2 hard-cooked eggs, chopped finely

⅓ cup mayonnaise

⅛ teaspoon hickory liquid smoke

⅛ teaspoon Tabasco sauce

Combine all ingredients and mix until well blended in mixer. Press into lightly oiled 2-cup mold or small loaf pan. Chill for at least 24 hours. Unmold. Serve with Melba toast or crackers.

ROLLED chicken sandwiches

9 ounces softened cream cheese
2 cups (firmly packed) finely
    ground cooked chicken
½ cup finely ground celery
¼ cup finely chopped parsley
½ cup white wine or 4
    tablespoons French dressing
1 teaspoon grated onion
1 teaspoon Worcestershire
    sauce
Softened butter or margarine
40 slices fresh white bread,
    crusts removed, rolled out
    thin with rolling pin.

Mix all ingredients for filling very thoroughly. Spread mixture on buttered bread slices. Roll up. Place on sheets, seam side down. Cover with damp towels. Refrigerate. May be cut in half for bite-sized servings. Serve on bed of parsley and garnish platters with cherry tomatoes or radishes.

chicken LIVER pâté

½ pound chicken livers
1 teaspoon salt
Pinch of cayenne pepper
½ cup softened butter
¼ teaspoon nutmeg
1 teaspoon dry mustard
⅛ teaspoon ground cloves
2 tablespoons finely ground onion

Wash and remove any loose fibers from chicken livers. Cover with water and bring to a boil. Cover and simmer for about 10 minutes. Drain and while livers are still hot put them through finest blade of a food chopper. Blend in remaining ingredients and mix very well. Chill thoroughly. The pâté may be packed into a crock or well-oiled mold. Serve with Melba rounds.

ROQUEFORT-FILLED
mushrooms

12 medium-sized, perfectly
    shaped mushroom caps
4 ounces Roquefort cheese
½ cup butter
½ teaspoon dry mustard
Finely chopped parsley
Toasted almond slivers

Carefully peel mushroom
caps. Mix together Roque-
fort cheese, butter, and dry
mustard. Stuff or pipe into
the mushrooms. Decorate
with almond slivers and
dust with chopped parsley.
Chill thoroughly on a covered
tray.

☆ Raw mushrooms and
Roquefort make a really
great combination!

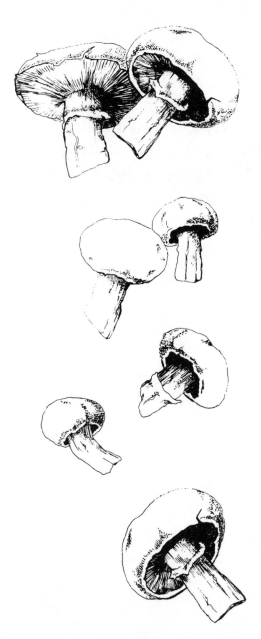

seafood STUFFED EGGS

8 hard-cooked eggs
½ cup mayonnaise
½ teaspoon salt
½ teaspoon curry powder
½ teaspoon paprika
¼ teaspoon dry mustard
1 cup chopped shrimp,
   lobster, or crabmeat

Peel and cut eggs in half. Remove yolks. Mash yolks thoroughly with mayonnaise and seasonings. Mix in finely chopped seafood. (Taste for seasoning. You may want more or less.) Stuff into egg whites. Dust with paprika. Nest on a plate of parsley. Cover with plastic wrap. Chill.

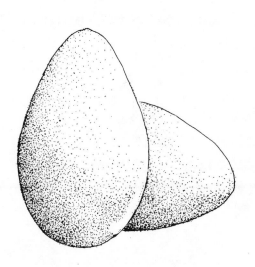

shrimp
páté mold

2 pounds shrimp, cooked
  and cleaned
3/4 cup softened butter
2 tablespoons lemon juice
1/2 teaspoon mace
1/2 teaspoon dry mustard
Few drops Tabasco sauce
Few drops Worcestershire
  sauce
1/2 teaspoon salt
2 tablespoons mayonnaise
  (optional)

Reserve a few shrimp for garnish and put remaining shrimp through meat grinder, using medium-fine blade. Blend remaining ingredients in very thoroughly. Pack firmly in well-oiled bowl or mold. Cover with plastic wrap and chill thoroughly. Unmold on chilled plate and garnish with reserved shrimp. Ring mold with parsley.

☆ Serve with crackers or crisp toast.

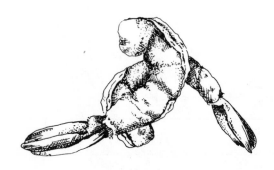

hot
main
dishes

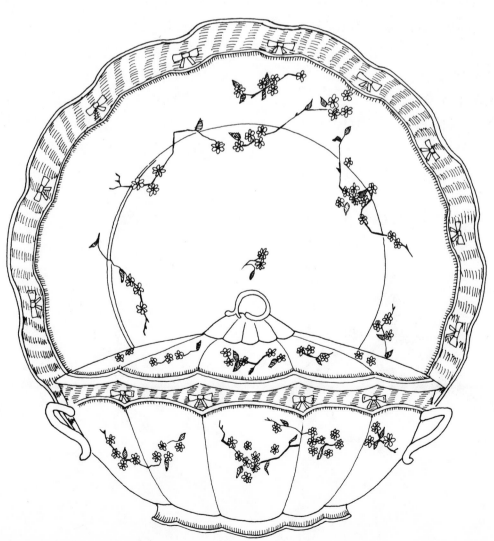

ROQUEFORT-STUFFED
MEATLOAF

1½ pounds ground round
    (or 1 pound ground round
    and ½ pound ground pork)
½ cup chopped onion
2 tablespoons chopped parsley

1 tablespoon salt
¼ teaspoon pepper
2 cups soft bread crumbs
1 egg
¼ cup catsup

Mix all ingredients together and pat out on 12 x 15-inch sheet of waxed paper. Spread with the following mixture:

4 cups cubed bread
¼ cup scalded milk

1 egg
1 cup crumbled Roquefort cheese

Roll up firmly lengthwise. Remove from paper. Place on lightly oiled baking sheet. Bake at 375°F. for 1 hour. To reheat: Cover with foil. Heat for 20 minutes at 325°F.

☆ This is a tasty dish served
either hot or cold.

SUBLIME SEAFOOD

¼ cup butter
3 tablespoons flour
1 cup milk
1 cup light cream
1 cup crushed Ritz crackers
¼ cup dry sherry
1 cup fresh crabmeat (or lobster or shrimp), finely cut
Salt and pepper to taste
¼ cup melted butter
Paprika

In a saucepan melt ¼ cup butter. Add flour, stirring until well blended and bubbly. Whisk in milk and cream and cook until smooth. Remove from heat and stir in sherry. Season lightly with salt and pepper. Add seafood. Pour into lightly buttered au gratin dish or individual shells. Blend together ¼ cup butter and cracker crumbs. Top seafood mixture with buttered crumbs and sprinkle with paprika. Bake at 350° F. for 15-20 minutes. Bake for an additional 15 minutes if mixture has been refrigerated. Serves 4.

☆ Please don't use canned seafood for this. The recipe deserves the best.

artichoke & shrimp
CASSEROLE

2 packages frozen artichoke hearts, slightly cooked and drained

2 pounds shrimp, cooked and cleaned

½ pound mushrooms

¼ cup butter

3 cups medium cream sauce

1½ tablespoons Worcestershire sauce

½ cup dry sherry

½ cup mixture of soft bread crumbs and Parmesan cheese

Salt, pepper, and paprika
Parsley

Line bottom of buttered oblong baking dish with artichokes. Sauté mushrooms in butter and place over artichokes. Arrange shrimp on mushroom layer. Add Worcestershire sauce and seasonings to cream sauce. Add sherry. Pour sauce over shrimp. Top with crumbs and sprinkle with paprika. Bake in 375°F. oven for 20 minutes. Sprinkle with finely chopped parsley or garnish with parsley sprigs.

BUFFET VEAL amandine

2 pounds lean veal, cubed
½ cup butter, divided
1 pound mushrooms, sliced
½ cup chopped onions
1 clove garlic, crushed
1 teaspoon salt
¼ teaspoon pepper
½ teaspoon rosemary
¼ cup flour
1 cup dry vermouth
1 cup water

Sauté veal cubes in ¼ cup butter. Sauté mushrooms in ¼ cup butter and reserve. Add onions and garlic to veal and brown lightly. Add seasonings and coat all with flour. Stirring mixture constantly over low heat, add vermouth and water. Stir in mushrooms. Cover and simmer very gently over low heat for about 2 hours, stirring occasionally. Add more vermouth if necessary. Spoon into serving dish and sprinkle with toasted almonds. May be reheated, covered, at 350° F. for 15-20 minutes.

chicken almond
SUPREME

6 cups cooked chicken, cut up
2 cups slivered, ligntly
   toasted almonds
½ cup butter
1 pound mushrooms, cleaned
   and sliced
½ cup flour
Salt and pepper
2½ cups chicken broth
1 cup light cream
½ cup dry sherry
1 cup soft bread crumbs
¼ cup melted butter
¼ cup Parmesan cheese
Paprika

Sauté mushrooms in ½ cup butter. Lower heat and add flour, salt, and pepper. Blend in broth, cream, and sherry. Add chicken. Add 1 cup almonds. Spoon into buttered casserole. Blend bread crumbs, ¼ cup melted butter, and Parmesan cheese. Spread over casserole. Sprinkle with remaining 1 cup almonds. Sprinkle with paprika. Bake at 350°F. for 20 minutes until bubbling and golden.

chicken & ham
MARYLAND

4 large chicken breasts, split

8 slices boiled or baked ham

8 slices firm white bread, crusts trimmed, sautéed in butter until golden

2 cups medium cream sauce

1 cup grated Sharp Cheddar Cheese

1 cup buttered soft bread crumbs

Salt and pepper

Paprika

Cover chicken with well-seasoned water and simmer until tender. Remove skin and bones leaving chicken intact. Place sautéed bread slices in shallow baking dish or pan. Place one slice of ham on each bread slice. Top with chicken. Blend cheese into cream sauce and season to taste. Pour sauce over chicken pieces. Top with buttered bread crumbs and paprika. Bake at 375°F. for about 15 minutes until golden and bubbling.

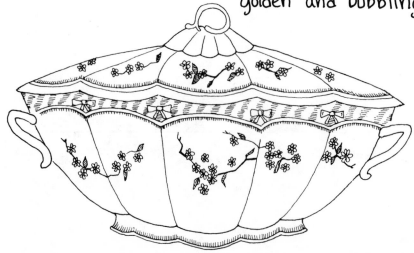

Stuffed Shells

1 (12 ounce) package jumbo
   pasta shells
2 packages frozen creamed
   spinach, thawed
1 (15 ounce) carton ricotta
   cheese
1 (8 ounce) package shredded
   Mozzarella cheese
1 teaspoon salt
1/4 teaspoon pepper
1/2 pound lean ground beef
1 (32 ounce) jar spaghetti
   sauce

This is for the "convenience food" lovers. You can certainly use your own sauce or creamed spinach or chop your own cheese if you wish.

Cook pasta as directed on the package, being careful not to overcook it. Brown beef in a skillet. Remove from heat. Add all remaining ingredients <u>except</u> sauce. Blend well. In a large baking dish put half of the spaghetti sauce. Fill shells with mixture and arrange rather closely in the dish. Pour remaining sauce over. Bake at 350°F. for 30 minutes until bubbling. Makes about 32 shells.

spaghetti sauce

½ pound Italian sweet
  Sausages
½ pound Italian hot sausages
1 pound spareribs, cut into
  small pieces
1 (28 ounce) can tomatoes
14 ounces tomato paste

1 onion, chopped
½ cup olive oil
1 tablespoon salt
1 tablespoon pepper
1 tablespoon sugar
2½ cups water
½ cup red wine

Sauté onion in olive oil until transparent. Add tomatoes, tomato paste, salt, pepper, and sugar. Bring to a boil, stirring. Reduce to a simmer. Stir in 2½ cups water. Slice sausages into bite-sized pieces. Brown in a skillet. Drain well. Add to sauce. In same skillet brown sparerib pieces. Drain and add to sauce. Make meatballs. Drop into simmering sauce. Cover and simmer for 1½ hours, stirring occasionally. Serve over 1 pound cooked spaghetti. Sprinkle with Parmesan cheese.

MEATBALLS

1 pound ground round
½ cup soft bread crumbs
1 egg beaten
½ teaspoon salt

1 tablespoon chopped parsley
3 tablespoons water
Flour
Vegetable oil

Mix together thoroughly. Form into balls. Roll lightly in flour. Fry in vegetable oil until lightly browned.

CURRIED EGGS NEWBURG

8 hard-cooked eggs (prepared and stuffed exactly as for Seafood Stuffed Eggs, page 19)
1/4 cup butter
3 tablespoons flour
1 cup milk
1 cup light cream
1/4 cup dry sherry
1 cup crab, shrimp, or lobster, cut up finely
Salt and pepper
1 cup crushed Ritz crackers
1/4 cup butter, melted
Paprika

Make a roux of 1/4 cup butter and flour over low heat. Whisk in milk and cream. Add sherry. Add seafood and season to taste. Arrange eggs in lightly buttered baking dish. Pour sauce over all. Mix together cracker crumbs and 1/4 cup melted butter. Sprinkle over eggs. Sprinkle with paprika. Bake at 350°F. for 15-20 minutes. Add 15 minutes baking time if casserole is refrigerated before baking.

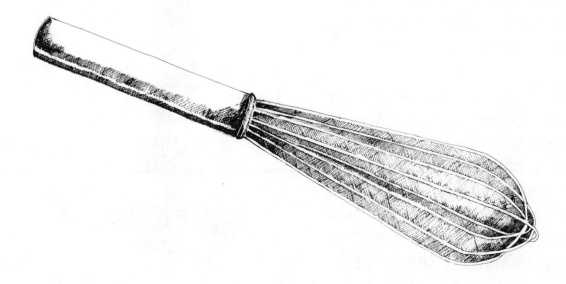

ham & asparagus
SUISSE

16 asparagus tips, partially
    cooked and drained
16 slices boiled ham
½ pound Swiss cheese, grated
2 cups medium cream sauce
Bread crumbs
Butter

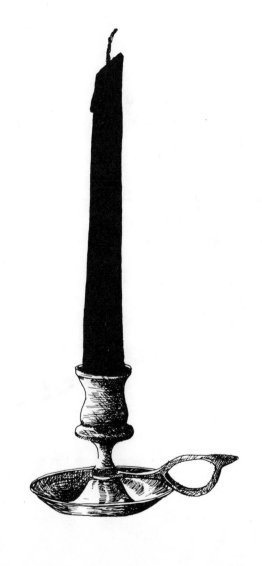

Roll each asparagus tip in a
slice of ham. Arrange rolls in
buttered baking dish. Over low
heat blend Swiss cheese into
cream sauce. Pour sauce over
rolls. Sprinkle with crumbs.
Dot with butter. Bake at 350°F.
until bubbling and browned.

☆ If you like, you may substi-
tute Belgian endive hearts for
asparagus. Poach them gently
in a half and half mixture of
water and white wine and 2
tablespoons lemon juice. Cook
endive hearts until they are
<u>barely</u> tender. Drain well.

ham & broccoli
CASSEROLE

¼ cup butter

1½ cups chopped onion

2 cups washed, chopped mushrooms

2 (10¾ ounce) cans cream of mushroom soup

1½ cups milk

3 packages frozen broccoli spears, cooked and drained

Salt and pepper

2 cups coarsley chopped ham

1½ cups herb-flavored stuffing mix

Melt butter and sauté onions and mushrooms until tender. Add soup and milk and mix well. Arrange one third of the broccoli in the bottom of a buttered casserole. Season. Layer the casserole using one third of the ham, one third of the stuffing mix, and one half of the sauce. Repeat until all are used ending with stuffing mix. Bake at 350° F. for about 30 minutes.

☆ Don't let this be too dry. You can always add a bit of liquid.

CRABMEAT QUICHE

1 (7 ounce) package frozen
  King crabmeat
¼ cup chopped scallions
  (use some green)
¼ cup chopped celery
⅛ cup chopped green pepper
2 tablespoons butter
4 eggs

1½ cups milk
1½ teaspoons dry mustard
½ teaspoon salt
¼ teaspoon nutmeg
¼ teaspoon pepper
1 egg white
1 10-inch unbaked pie shell

Thaw, drain, and flake crabmeat. Sauté scallions, celery, and green pepper in butter. In a large bowl beat eggs slightly. Add milk and seasonings. Blend well. Add crabmeat and vegetable mixture. Beat egg white slightly and brush pie shell with it. Chill. Pour egg mixture into shell. Bake in pre-heated 375°F. oven for 40 minutes until filling is puffed and brown. Cool in pan for at least 15 minutes before cutting. Serves 6-8. This may be frozen and reheated.

spinach quiche

3½ cups flour
2½ teaspoons salt
3/4 cups butter or margarine
7 eggs
7 tablespoons cold water
½ teaspoon pepper
½ teaspoon nutmeg

2 cups shredded Swiss cheese
1 package frozen spinach, thawed and drained
2 cups whipping cream
2 cups milk
1 medium onion minced

In a large bowl combine 3 cups of the flour with 1 teaspoon salt. Cut in the butter with a pastry blender. Add 1 egg, slightly beaten with the water. Roll out into a large rectangle to fit 15 x 10-inch jelly roll pan. Crimp edges. Chill. Sprinkle cheese and spinach over bottom of the crust. In a large bowl combine 6 eggs, cream, milk, onion, ½ cup flour, 1½ teaspoons salt, pepper, and nutmeg. Mix well. Pour over cheese and spinach. Bake in a preheated 400°F. oven for 35-40 minutes. Serves 12 as a main course or makes 48 bite-sized pieces. This may be made ahead. Refrigerate, covered, and reheat in 425°F. oven for 10 minutes.

LAzy man's
LOBSTER

☆ For 6 lazy lobster fans
6 boiled lobsters
1 cup butter
⅓ cup lemon juice
½ teaspoon salt
½ teaspoon pepper
3 tablespoons melted butter
¼ cup sherry
1 cup soft bread crumbs

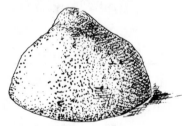

Butter 1 large or 6 individual casseroles. Remove lobster from shells and put large pieces into casserole (don't forget the tamale and coral). Melt 1 cup butter and combine with lemon juice and seasonings. Pour over lobster. Combine 3 tablespoons melted butter with sherry and pour over bread crumbs. Toss mixture well. Sprinkle crumbs over the lobsters. Cover tightly. Bake at 400°F. for 20 minutes.

☆ Cut butter mixture in half if you want less richness.

RAGOUT OF BEEF
& RED WINE

2 pounds lean round or top
    sirloin, cut into cubes
1 large clove garlic, minced
2 medium onions, chopped
3 tablespoons salad oil
Flour
Salt and pepper
Rosemary
Dry red wine

In an electric skillet or flame-proof casserole brown meat, onions, and garlic in oil. When meat is browned, add enough flour to coat thoroughly. Mix well. Add salt, pepper, and 1/4 - 1/2 teaspoon rosemary. Cover with wine. Cover pan or casserole and cook at low heat (or in 275°F. oven) until meat is very tender. Add more wine if necessary but do not add water. Just keep it bubbling gently. Serve over noodles or rice. This keeps beautifully. To reheat: Cover and simmer gently. This ragout also freezes well.

WELSH RABBIT BAKE

1 (1 pound) loaf rye bread, sliced, (crusts off)
12 ounces sliced, sharp Cheddar cheese
3 cups milk
1 (12 ounce) can beer or ale
6 eggs
2 teaspoons Worcestershire sauce
1 teaspoon salt
1 teaspoon dry mustard
¼ teaspoon freshly ground black pepper
2 tablespoons melted butter

Butter a 13x9x2-inch baking dish. Layer the bread and cheese in dish and top with cheese. Beat together all remaining ingredients except butter. Pour over bread and cheese. Drizzle with butter. Cover and refrigerate at least an hour or overnight. Bake in preheated 350°F. oven for 60-70 minutes until bubbly and puffed. Let stand for at least 5 minutes before serving. Serves 6-8.

SOLE WITH SOUL

6 large fillets of sole
1 cup sliced mushrooms
2 shallots, minced
1 tablespoon minced parsley
1 cup white wine
1 cup bottled clam juice
Salt and pepper
3 tablespoons flour
3 tablespoons soft butter
2 cups crabmeat
Green seedless grapes

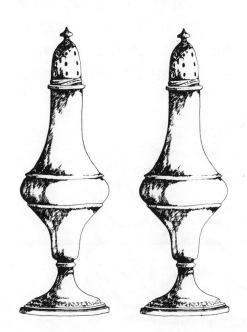

In a large skillet simmer mushrooms, shallots, wine, and clam juice for about 5 minutes. Remove from heat and lay fish fillets in mixture in a single layer. Return to heat and poach gently for only a few minutes. DO NOT LET FISH GET SOFT! Remove fish gently with slotted spatula, draining well. Lay in well-buttered au gratin dish or oblong casserole. Season. Reduce pan juices to about 1½ cups. Blend flour and butter and add to pan juices. Stir until smooth and boiling. Stir In crabmeat. Pour over fish. Wreath edges of dish with green grapes. Glaze under broiler at medium heat until bubbling and slightly browned or bake at 450°F. for 5-10 minutes.

SCALLOP SURPRISE

4 cups raw sliced potatoes
½ cup thinly sliced green
   pepper
2 cups thinly sliced onion
1 pound scallops (cut if
   large)
¼ cup butter
3 tablespoons flour
2 cups milk
½ teaspoon salt
⅛ teaspoon pepper
1 cup bread crumbs
2 tablespoons melted butter

Boil potatoes, onions, and peppers until barely tender. Drain. Place in buttered casserole. Sauté well-drained scallops in ¼ cup butter. Add flour, stirring gently. Add milk. Bring to a boil. Add seasonings. Pour over potato mixture. Blend gently. Mix bread crumbs with 2 tablespoons melted butter and use as a topping. Bake at 400°F. for 20 minutes. Serves 6. May be reheated, covered, at 400°F. until gently bubbling.

STEAK & KIDNEY PIE

6 lamb kidneys, deveined and cut up
¼ cup butter
½ pound mushrooms, sliced
2 tablespoons Worcestershire sauce
1 recipe Ragout of Beef, page 37
Pastry
1 egg
Paprika

Over medium heat in a large skillet sauté kidneys in butter. Add mushrooms. Stir and cook until browned. Add Beef Ragout and Worcestershire sauce. Blend well. Pour into a 3-quart oblong Pyrex dish. Cool. Roll out pastry to fit top giving 1-inch excess at edges. Place on dish and crimp firmly. Slash in several places. Brush with egg wash (1 egg and 2 tablespoons water). Decorate with trimmings of pastry cut into shapes. Brush again with egg. Sprinkle with paprika. Bake at 375°F. for 1 hour or at 425°F. until brown and 325°F. for additional 10 minutes.

PASTRY

2 cups flour
1 teaspoon salt
⅔ cup plus 4 tablespoons margarine
¼ cup water

Blend flour, salt, and margarine with pastry blender. Add water. Blend and knead slightly. Chill.

41

almond crust
macaroni

2 (14¾ ounce) cans macaroni
  in cheese sauce
1 teaspoon Worcestershire
  sauce
1 tablespoon instant minced
  onion
¼ teaspoon hot powdered
  mustard
½ cup slivered, blanched
  almonds
½ cup grated Cheddar cheese

Combine macaroni, Worcestershire sauce, onion, and mustard. Mix well. Spoon into well—buttered au gratin pan or shallow Pyrex dish. Sprinkle almonds and cheese over the surface. Bake in preheated 350° F. oven for 20-25 minutes or until bubbling. Serves 6.

cold
main
dishes

salmon mousse

1 envelope plus 1 teaspoon
   plain gelatin
2 tablespoons lemon juice
1 teaspoon dill seed
1/4 teaspoon paprika
1/2 teaspoon salt
1/2 cup boiling water
1/2 cup mayonnaise
1 small onion, peeled and
   sliced
1 stalk celery, washed and
   cut up
1 (1 pound) can salmon, with
   broth
2 tablespoons coarsely cut
   pimento
1 cup heavy cream
1 egg

In a blender container place gelatin, lemon juice, dill seed, paprika, salt, and water. Cover and blend at high speed for about 40 seconds. Turn off motor. Add mayonnaise, onion, celery, salmon, pimento, cream, and egg. Cover and blend on low speed for about 10 seconds. Stop when salmon is coarsely chopped. Pour into oiled 1 1/2-quart mold. Chill until really firm. Unmold. Garnish as desired. Serve with sour cream.

☆ Great as a first course.
   Double recipe for a buffet.

LIME RING
with
shrimp & avocado

3 (3 ounce) packages lime-
  flavored gelatin
3   cups hot water
2 1/4 cups cold water
6 tablespoons vinegar
6 tablespoons mayonnaise
1 tablespoon finely chopped
  onion
3 cups small-curd cottage
  cheese
3   nicely ripened avocados
Lemon juice
3 pounds shrimp, cooked
  and cleaned
Bibb lettuce, washed, dried,
  and separated

Dissolve gelatin in hot water.
Add cold water and vinegar.
Chill until slightly thickened.
Combine mayonnaise, onion,
and cottage cheese. Mix well.
Gradually add gelatin, blending
well. Pour into a 3-quart
ring mold. Chill until firm,
at least 4 or 5 hours. Peel
and slice avocados. Sprinkle
with lemon juice. Remove
gelatin to cold plate lined
with lettuce. Pile avocados
in center of gelatin. Surround with shrimp. Serve
with Blender Mayonnaise,
page 76.

TUNA-CUCUMBER MOUSSE

1 tablespoon plain gelatin
¼ cup cold water
1 (10½ ounce) can condensed
    cream of chicken soup
1 (7 ounce) can solid-pack
    tuna, drained and flaked
1 teaspoon grated onion
⅛ teaspoon salt
1 tablespoon lemon juice
¼ cup mayonnaise
1½ cups cucumber, unpeeled
    and finely chopped

Soften gelatin in water. Heat soup to boiling point. Stir in gelatin thoroughly. Remove from heat. Add tuna. Add onion, salt, and lemon juice. Cool. Add mayonnaise and cucumber. Blend. Pour into oiled 1-quart mold, fish-shaped if possible. Chill until really firm. Unmold on greens. Garnish with parsley and lemon wedges.

RAGGEDY ANN
SALADS

2 hard-cooked eggs, halved
   lengthwise
Whole cloves
1 small jar pimentos
Carrot shavings
2 medium, firm tomatoes,
   peeled and halved
4 cups chicken salad
4 large lettuce leaves
8 long strips of green pepper

Assemble each Raggedy Ann
as follows: ½ hard cooked egg
is the head; use cloves for the
eyes and pimento bits for the
nose and mouth. Place carrot
shavings around the top and
sides of the egg to make the
hair. Place a tomato half to
form the body. Arrange 1 cup
chicken salad to form the
skirt and cover with a lettuce
leaf. Form arms with green
pepper strips. Use pimento
strips, peeping out from the
lettuce leaf, to form feet. Serve
well chilled with a bowl of
curried mayonnaise.

easy chaud-froid chicken

6 cooked chicken breast halves, boned, skinned and chilled

1½ cups rich, well-flavored chicken broth

1½ teaspoons unflavored gelatin

½ cup cold water

½ teaspoon curry powder (or more if you like)

⅓ cup mayonnaise

Soften gelatin in ½ cup cold water. Heat chicken broth to boiling and add gelatin mixture. Add curry powder. Pour into a Pyrex cup or pitcher and cool. Put mayonnaise into a bowl and gradually whisk in cooled broth a bit at a time, blending until smooth. Chill until mixture begins to set. Place chicken breasts on a wire rack over a pan (to catch drippings). Spoon glaze over chicken, covering pieces well. Chill well. Decorate with sliced black olives. Serves 6.

☆ This same sauce, without the curry, is great for covering poached salmon steaks. Decorate with capers.

CURRIED SHRIMP MOLD WITH MELON

3 tablespoons butter
1 small onion, finely chopped
2 tablespoons unflavored gelatin
1 cup water
2 tablespoons curry powder
1/3 cup sugar
3 tablespoons vinegar
1 1/2 teaspoons salt
1/4 teaspoon ground ginger
1 chicken bouillon cube
2 cups plain yogurt
2 cups chopped, cooked shrimp
1 ripe cantaloupe, cut into melon balls

Simmer onion in butter until soft. Soften gelatin in 1 cup water. Add curry powder, sugar, vinegar, salt, ginger, and gelatin mixture to onion. Add bouillon cube and mix well. Remove from heat and cool until mixture starts to set. Fold in yogurt and shrimp. Pour into 1-quart lightly oiled mold. Chill overnight. Unmold on Boston lettuce. Surround with melon balls (honey dew can be substituted for part of the cantaloupe). Serve with mayonnaise to which chopped chutney has been added. Serves 6.

JELLIED chicken avocado

2 tablespoons unflavored gelatin
3½ cups chicken broth
1 tablespoon lemon juice
1 teaspoon grated onion

Salt and pepper to taste
1 avocado, ripe but firm
2 cups diced, cooked chicken
1 cup finely diced celery
pimento strips

Soften gelatin in 1 cup cold chicken broth. Heat remaining 2½ cups chicken broth until boiling. Remove from heat. Add gelatin mixture, lemon juice, onion, salt, and pepper. Chill mixture until it just starts to set. Pour about ½ cup of mixture into bottom of a 6-cup mold. Chill until set. Do not chill remaining mixture. Peel avocado and cut half of it into thin strips lengthwise. Arrange these strips in pinwheel fashion on set gelatin. Outline edge of each slice with pimento strips. Spoon a little of the remaining gelatin mixture over these and chill to set. Dice remaining avocado. Add avocado, chicken, and celery to remaining gelatin mixture. Pour into mold. Chill until firm. Unmold and garnish with celery leaves and radish roses. Serves 8.

☆ To retain bright avocado color, toss slices and
diced pieces in a bit of lemon juice.
I like to serve this with the following dressing:
3/4 cup mayonnaise
1/4 teaspoon curry powder
2 teaspoons lemon juice

chicken loaf

2 egg yolks, slightly beaten
½ teaspoon salt
¼ teaspoon paprika
1 cup chicken broth
1 tablespoon unflavored gelatin
¼ cup cold water
1 cup finely diced cooked chicken
1 teaspoon horseradish
½ teaspoon Worcestershire
   sauce
1 cup heavy cream, whipped
½ cup mayonnaise

Dissolve gelatin in cold water. In the top of a double boiler combine egg yolks, salt, paprika, and chicken broth. Cook over simmering hot water, stirring constantly, for about 15 minutes or until slightly thickened. Add gelatin mixture and blend well. Cool and chill until mixture begins to set (becomes quaky). Fold in remaining ingredients. When blended put into a lightly oiled loaf pan. Chill overnight. Turn out onto a platter and garnish as desired. Serves 6.

vegetables

DIVINE POTATOES

1 (10½ ounce) can cream of celery or cream of chicken soup

½ cup milk

1 (3 ounce) package cream cheese

4 cups frozen hash brown potatoes

1 cup frozen small whole onions

Salt and pepper to taste

½ cup shredded sharp Cheddar cheese

Combine in a saucepan soup, milk, and cream cheese. Heat and stir until smooth. Add potatoes and onions and season to taste. Pour mixture into a 2-quart (preferably oblong) buttered casserole. Cover with foil or a lid. Bake for 1¼ hours at 350°F. Remove cover. Top with cheese. Return to oven for about 7 minutes to melt cheese. This reheats beautifully, uncovered, at 325°F. for 15-20 minutes.

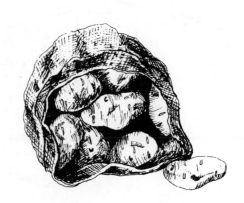

BROCCOLI
ALMOST-SOUFFLÉ

1/4 cup finely chopped onion
1/4 cup butter
2 tablespoons flour
1/2 cup water
1 (8 ounce) jar Cheez-Whiz
2 packages chopped frozen broccoli, thawed
3 eggs, well-beaten
1/2 cup crushed Ritz crackers
2 tablespoons melted butter
Grated Parmesan cheese

Sauté onion in 1/4 cup butter until soft. Stir in flour. Add water and cook until thickened. Add Cheez-Whiz. Blend well until smooth. Remove from heat. Add well-drained broccoli. Stir in eggs and blend gently. Pour into well-buttered 1 1/2-quart casserole. Combine crackers, butter, and Parmesan cheese. Sprinkle over casserole. Bake at 325°F. for 40 minutes or refrigerate and bake later for 1 hour. May be frozen after baking.

corn & onion
pie

1 9-inch unbaked pie shell
2 tablespoons butter
1 cup milk
2 cups fresh corn kernels, drained
3 tablespoons chopped green pepper
1 teaspoon sugar
1/4 cup heavy cream
1 teaspoon salt
1/8 teaspoon pepper
3 tablespoons soft bread crumbs
2 eggs, well beaten
1 (3 ounce) can French fried onions (crisped in oven)
1/3 cup buttered cracker crumbs

In a saucepan combine butter, milk, corn, green pepper, and sugar. Bring to a boil and then simmer for a few minutes. Slowly stir in cream. Add salt, pepper, and bread crumbs. Cook until thickened. Cool slightly. Stir in eggs. Pour one half of mixture into pie shell. Cover with onions. Add remaining corn mixture. Top with buttered crumbs. Bake at 400° F. for 20-25 minutes. May be reheated at 350° F. for 15 minutes.

GREEN BEANS
with mushrooms

2 packages frozen French-style green beans

2 (1 3/8 ounce) envelopes cheese sauce mix

1 (6 ounce or more) can sliced mushrooms

2 tablespoons chopped pimento

1 (5 ounce) can water chestnuts, drained and sliced

Cook beans until <u>almost</u> done. Drain well. Prepare cheese sauce mix according to package directions. Add remaining ingredients. Pour into buttered 1½-quart casserole. Bake at 350°F. for 15 minutes until bubbling.

EGGPLANT-TOMATO SUPREME

2 medium eggplants
Salt
Olive oil or cooking oil
Freshly ground pepper
1 cup grated Parmesan
   Cheese
2/3 cup heavy cream
6 tomatoes, peeled and
   sliced
Buttered bread crumbs
Melted butter

Peel eggplant and slice thin. Sprinkle with salt and let stand for 1 hour. Drain and wipe. Fry slices in oil until golden. Drain. Butter a deep 3-quart casserole. Place a layer of eggplant in the bottom of the casserole. Sprinkle with pepper, grated cheese, and cream. Add a layer of tomatoes, pepper, cheese, and cream. Repeat until casserole is filled, ending with cream. Top with buttered crumbs and cheese. Drizzle with melted butter. Bake at 375° F. for 45 minutes. Reheat at 350° F. for 20 minutes if desired.

GINGER SPINACH

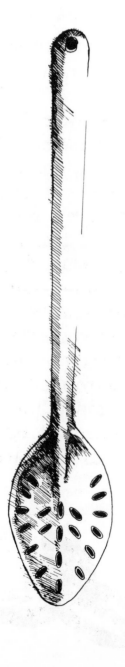

3 packages chopped frozen
  spinach
1 (10½ ounce) can cream of
  mushroom soup
1 cup sour cream
1 generous teaspoon ground
  ginger
½ teaspoon prepared mustard
Salt and pepper
1 (3 ounce) can French fried
  onions

Cook spinach in ½ cup water
for 5 minutes, covered.
Drain well, pressing all juice
out of spinach. In a large
bowl mix spinach with re-
maining ingredients, reserv-
ing a few onions. Pour into
greased 1½-quart casserole.
Garnish top with reserved
onions. Bake in preheated
350°F. oven for 30-40
minutes.

LIMA BEANS
AT THEIR BEST

8 slices bacon, fried, drained,
  and crumbled
1 medium onion, chopped
2 packages frozen lima
  beans, cooked and drained
1 (10½ ounce) can mush-
  room soup
1 pint dairy sour cream
Salt and pepper

Mix all ingredients together,
thoroughly and gently. Pour
into a 2- quart buttered
casserole. Cover. Bake at
350°F. for 30-40 minutes.
This reheats easily at 325°F.
for 20 minutes, covered.

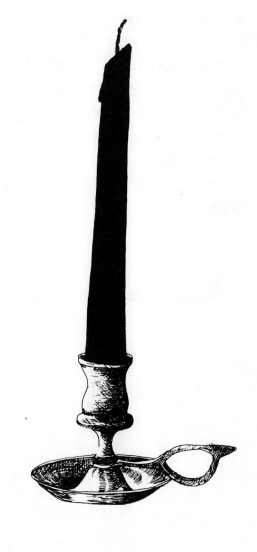

RED CABBAGE
à la polonaise

1 large red cabbage, shredded
3 small onions, finely chopped
2 apples, diced
1 cup currant jelly
3 tablespoons vinegar
1/3 cup seedless raisins
A few caraway seeds
3 tablespoons butter
2 cloves
2 peppercorns
Salt

Rinse cabbage. Put into a large pan with one inch of water. Bring to a simmer. Stir in remaining ingredients. Stir. Cook covered for 1 - 1 1/2 hours, stirring occasionally. Remove cloves and peppercorns. Add salt to taste. Serves 8.

JELLIED CIDER
WALDORF RING

2 tablespoons unflavored gelatin
½ cup cold cider
3½ cups hot cider
1 tablespoon sugar
½ stick cinnamon
2 whole cloves

2 cups diced McIntosh apples
1 cup chopped celery
½ cup chopped walnuts or
    pecans
⅛ teaspoon nutmeg
Juice of half a lemon

    Soften gelatin and 1 tablespoon sugar in cold cider. In a saucepan heat 3½ cups cider with cinnamon and cloves until boiling. Remove from heat. Remove spices. Stir in softened gelatin. Stir until dissolved. Cool until mixture starts to thicken but not set. In a bowl mix apples (peeled or not), celery, and nuts. Toss with nutmeg and lemon juice. Pour into thickened cider mixture. Blend. Pour into 6½-cup ring mold. Chill well. Serve with mixture of mayonnaise and sour cream as a dressing. I sometimes substitute ½ cup seeded and halved red grapes for ½ cup of the apples. Garnish as desired. Serves 10-12.

ROSÉ WINE MOLD

1 pound seedless grapes
3 tablespoons gelatin
¾ cup sugar
3 cups rosé wine
1 cup water

Stem and halve about 35 grapes. Leave the remaining grapes in small bunches for garnish. Sprinkle gelatin over 1 cup water in a saucepan. Add sugar. Heat gently, stirring until dissolved. Remove from heat. Add wine. Cool until mixture starts to thicken. Fold in grapes and pour into a lightly oiled 6-cup mold. Chill until firm. Unmold and garnish with remaining grapes.

a different Tossed salad

2 packages frozen green peas
1 cup thinly sliced radishes
1 cup thinly sliced red onions
2 quarts crisp mixed lettuces,
 washed, drained, and torn
French dressing

Cook peas until almost done.
Drain well. Cool in cold water
and drain well. Lightly mix
peas with remaining ingredients. Chill until ready to
serve. Toss thoroughly with
your favorite dressing or
mine:

French dressing

1 cup olive oil
⅓ cup wine vinegar
1 teaspoon salt
¼ teaspoon freshly ground
 pepper
1 clove garlic, gashed

Combine all ingredients and
shake well. Store in a tightly
closed container.

JELLIED GAZPACHO

1 tablespoon unflavored gelatin,
  dissolved in ½ cup water

1 cup beef bouillon

⅓ cup vinegar

1 teaspoon paprika

¼ teaspoon ground cloves

1 clove garlic, mashed

¼ cup chopped celery

1½ cups chopped tomatoes, drained

1 teaspoon salt

½ teaspoon basil

⅛ teaspoon Tabasco sauce

1 tablespoon chopped onion

½ cup chopped green pepper

Add softened gelatin to hot bouillon. Stir until well dissolved. Add all other ingredients. Mix well. Chill until mixture thickens. Pour into a 4-cup mold. Chill until firm. Unmold and garnish with lettuce. I serve this with a mixture of half mayonnaise and half sour cream as a dressing.

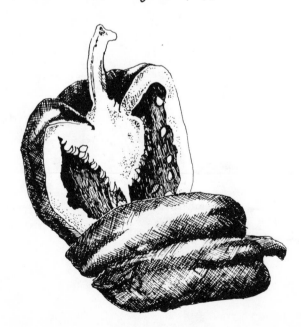

plain & fancy
potato
salad

plain

4 cups sliced, cooked potatoes
½ cup chopped scallions
  (use part green)
¼ cup chopped green pepper
2 hard-cooked eggs, chopped
¼ cup well-seasoned oil and
  vinegar dressing
¼ teaspoon dried dill weed
½ cup mayonnaise
½ cup sour cream
1 tablespoon Dijon mustard
1 teaspoon salt
¼ teaspoon black pepper

In a large bowl gently toss warm potatoes in oil and vinegar dressing and dill weed. Cool. Mix together mayonnaise, sour cream, mustard, salt, and pepper and add to potatoes. Add scallions, green pepper, and eggs. Toss gently. Chill thoroughly. Serves 6.

fancy

Firmly pack salad into loaf pan. Chill for 2 hours. Unmold and glaze.

glaze

1 envelope unflavored gelatin
½ cup cold chicken broth
1 cup mayonnaise

Sprinkle gelatin over broth in a small saucepan. Dissolve over low heat. Remove and stir in mayonnaise. Let stand for about 10 minutes. Spoon one half of glaze over top and sides of loaf. Let stand. Spoon remaining glaze over top and sides. Chill after applying desired decorations.

zucchini mousse

2 envelopes unflavored gelatin
1 cup cold water
¼ cup vinegar
2/3 cup mayonnaise
¾ teaspoon salt
⅛ teaspoon pepper
2 cups shredded, unpeeled
   zucchini, drained
1 cup heavy cream, whipped
1 tablespoon grated onion

In a saucepan soften gelatin in water and vinegar. Stir over low heat until dissolved. Cool. Gradually add gelatin to mayonnaise, salt, and pepper. Mix well. Chill until partially set. Fold in zucchini, whipped cream, and onion. Pour into lightly oiled 5-cup mold. Chill until firm. Unmold and garnish as desired. I like to use egg slices and green peppers.

GREEN BEAN SALAD

2 (1 pound) cans green beans, drained (or freshly cooked, drained green beans)
1 onion, peeled and thinly sliced
½ green pepper, julienne
⅛ teaspoon oregano
⅛ teaspoon dill
⅛ teaspoon basil
¼ teaspoon celery salt
1 clove garlic, peeled and crushed
¼ cup red wine vinegar
¼ cup olive oil
Salt and pepper to taste.

Put all ingredients into a bowl. Toss thoroughly. Cover and chill for at least 2 hours, tossing occasionally. Serve very cold. This keeps well.

avocado ribbon
aspic

This is a three-layer loaf.

First layer:
    Soften 1 envelope unflavored gelatin in 1/4 cup cold water. Add 1/2 cup boiling water, 1 teaspoon salt, 3 tablespoons lemon juice, and a few drops of Tabasco sauce. Cool until thick. Stir in 1 1/2 cups sieved ripe avocado (1 large or 1 1/2 small). Add a drop or so of green food coloring. Pour into oiled loaf pan. Chill.

Second layer:
    Soften 2 teaspoons unflavored gelatin in 1/4 cup cold water. Dissolve over hot water Mix. Combine 12 ounces cream cheese with 1/2 cup milk. Blend in 1 teaspoon salt, 2/3 cup mayonnaise, and 1/4 teaspoon Worcestershire sauce. Stir in gelatin. Spread over layer 1. Chill.

Third layer:
    Simmer 3 cups tomato juice with 1/2 bay leaf, 2 cloves, 2 sprigs parsley, 1 celery stalk, 3/4 teaspoon salt, and a dash cayenne for 5-7 minutes. Strain. Soften 1 1/2 envelopes unflavored gelatin in 1/3 cup cold water. Add to hot tomato juice. Add 1 1/2 tablespoons vinegar and 1 1/2 teaspoons grated onion. Chill until thickened and pour over cheese layer.

Chill loaf for several hours until really set. Unmold on crisp greens and serve with fresh mayonnaise. See my recipe for Blender Mayonnaise, page 76.

tangerine cheese salad

1 (3 ounce) package lemon
  gelatin
1 cup hot water
1 (3 ounce) package cream
  cheese, softened
1 (11 ounce) can mandarin
  oranges, drained
1 (6 ounce) can frozen
  tangerine juice

Dissolve gelatin in hot water.
Add tangerine juice (frozen)
and stir until well blended.
Add cream cheese. Blend
well in blender or food processor until smooth. Chill
until mixture starts to thick-
en. Fold in mandarin oranges.
Pour into lightly oiled 2½-
cup mold. Chill well. Unmold
and garnish with additional
fruit if desired.

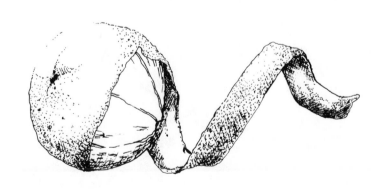

GREEK salad

1 teaspoon salt
2 cloves garlic, split
2 heads Boston lettuce
1 head romaine lettuce, shredded
6 radishes, sliced
1 bunch scallions, chopped
1 cucumber, sliced
12 Greek olives
1 cup crumbled Feta cheese
8 anchovy fillets (optional)
1 green pepper, sliced
3 tomatoes, cut in wedges

Rub a large salad bowl with salt and garlic. Discard garlic. Combine all other ingredients. Toss in dressing of:
¼ cup olive oil beaten with juice of 2 lemons
Season with freshly ground black pepper and ½ teaspoon oregano. Toss again. Sprinkle with one tablespoon chopped parsley.

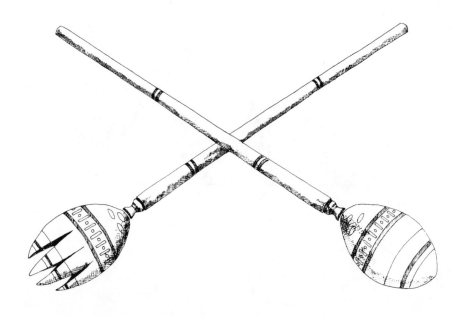

JELLIED BEETS

1 (3 ounce) package lemon
  gelatin
1 cup boiling water
1 teaspoon salt
2 tablespoons horseradish
2 tablespoons vinegar
1 tablespoon chopped onion
½ cup beet liquid
1½ cups diced beets

Prepare lemon gelatin with water. Stir in other ingredients except beets. Chill until thickened. Fold in beets. Spoon into a well-rinsed or lightly oiled mold. Chill thoroughly. Turn out onto chilled plate. Garnish as desired. Serve with dressing of equal proportions of sour cream and mayonnaise, well blended.

BLENDER MAYONNAISE

1 egg
2 tablespoons vinegar
½ teaspoon dry mustard
¼ teaspoon salt
1 cup salad oil
Few drops Tabasco sauce

Put egg, vinegar, mustard, salt, and ¼ cup of the oil in blender container. Blend for about 15 seconds at low speed. With blender still going add remaining oil and Tabasco sauce. Blend another 15 seconds. Replace cover. Turn on high and blend quickly until thick and well mixed.

bread

FEATHER-LIGHT MUFFINS

1 cup cake flour
⅓ cup sugar
1 egg
2 rounded teaspoons baking powder
½ teaspoon salt
½ cup milk
3 tablespoons melted butter

Sift dry ingredients together. Beat egg and milk together. Combine all, plus melted butter, and mix only enough to produce almost smooth batter. Spoon into well-buttered tins, one half full only. Bake at 375° F. for 15-20 minutes. Reheat, in foil-covered pan, at 400° F. for 10 minutes.

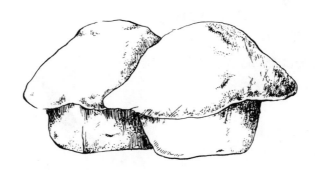

onion shortcake

8 medium onions, sliced thinly
1 recipe biscuit mix
1 egg
1 pint dairy sour cream

Cook onions in butter, slowly,
until transparent but not
brown. Roll out biscuit dough
1/2 inch thick. Place in square
baking pan. Spread over with
onions. Mix egg and sour
cream; then pour on onions.
Bake for 15-20 minutes
at 450°F. Reheats well at
400°F. for 10 minutes.

Great with steak!

ORANGE NUT BREAD

1 cup orange juice
Grated rind from 2 oranges
½ cup chopped walnuts
½ cup raisins
1 egg, well beaten
3 tablespoons melted shortening
1 teaspoon vanilla
½ cup sugar
2 cups all purpose flour
½ teaspoon baking soda
2 teaspoons baking powder
¼ teaspoon salt

Combine first 7 ingredients in large bowl. Sift dry ingredients together. Add to first 7 ingredients. Stir until blended. Pour into well-greased 9 x 5 x 3-inch loaf pan. Bake at 350° F. for 1 hour. Remove and cool. Wrap and chill in refrigerator. Slice thinly.

Great for tea sandwiches. Spread with butter or cream cheese.

WONDERFUL CORN BREAD

1 ½ cups yellow corn meal
1 cup flour
1 tablespoon baking powder
¼ cup sugar
1 teaspoon salt
¾ cup melted butter, cooled
2 eggs
1½ cups milk
1 cup corn, cooked and
   drained (optional)

Sift together dry ingredients.
Add butter, eggs, and milk.
Blend until just combined.
Add cooked corn if desired.
Pour into buttered 9-inch
square tin. Bake at 375°F.
for 40-45 minutes. May be
reheated, covered, at 350°F.
for 10 minutes.

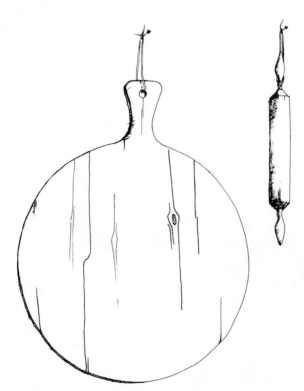

squash muffins

1 ¾ cups flour
½ teaspoon salt
2 teaspoons cream of tartar
1 teaspoon baking soda
4 tablespoons sugar
1 egg
½ cup milk
½ cup cooked and mashed
   squash
4 tablespoons melted shortening

Sift dry ingredients together. Beat egg and milk together and add to dry ingredients. Add squash. Add shortening. Mix again. Pour into well-buttered muffin tins. Bake at 375° F. for about 20 minutes. Turn out of tins immediately. Makes 12. To reheat, wrap in foil and bake at 350° F. for 10 minutes.

☆ These muffins freeze well.

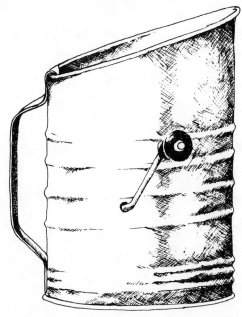

pull-apart coffee cake

2 (1 pound) loaves frozen bread dough
1 cup melted butter or margarine
1½ cups sugar
2 teaspoons cinnamon
1 cup chopped pecans

Defrost dough as directed on package. Shape into small balls the size of cherry tomatoes. Butter a large tube pan. Roll each ball in butter, then in sugar and cinnamon mixture, then in nuts. Fill tube pan with prepared balls, leaving space for expansion. Cover and allow to rise in a warm place for about 1 hour. Bake at 350°F. for 30-40 minutes. To reheat, remove from pan, cover with foil and heat at 350°F. for 20 minutes. Do not slice. Pull apart.

This freezes well.

desserts

divine
triple chocolate
pie

1 tablespoon unflavored gelatin
½ cup sugar
Dash of salt
1 tablespoon instant coffee
1 cup milk
3 eggs, separated

3 squares chocolate
1 teaspoon vanilla
¼ teaspoon cream of tartar
2 cups heavy cream
1 square chocolate, grated
1 (10-inch) chocolate cookie
crust (See Grasshopper
Pie, page 110)

In a heavy saucepan mix gelatin, ¼ cup sugar, salt, and instant coffee. Blend in milk, egg yolks, and 3 squares chocolate. Heat slowly over medium heat, stirring constantly with whisk. Do not boil. When smooth and almost boiling, remove from heat and add vanilla. Cool. Beat egg whites and cream of tartar until frothy. Slowly beat in remaining ¼ cup sugar. Beat until stiff. Beat one cup cream until stiff. Fold egg whites into chocolate mixture. Fold in whipped cream. Pour into pie shell. Chill until firm. Top with remaining cream, whipped. Sprinkle with grated chocolate. Chill.

☆ This pie really is divine. It was developed by a wonderful pastry chef who worked with me in New Hampshire.

steamed fig newton pudding

32 ounces fig newtons
1/2 cup coarsely chopped walnuts
3/4 cup milk
1/4 cup brandy
1/2 cup butter
2 eggs

2 teaspoons cinnamon
1/2 teaspoon ground cloves
1/2 teaspoon nutmeg
2 teaspoons lemon juice
2 tablespoons baking powder
1 teaspoon grated lemon rind

Break fig newtons into small pieces. Add nuts. Add combined milk and brandy. Stir. Let stand for 15 minutes. In mixer bowl cream butter. Add eggs. Beat well. Add spices, lemon juice, and baking powder. Beat well (mixture will look curdled). Add lemon rind and fig mixture. Blend well. Pour batter into greased 1 1/2 - quart mold. Cover tightly. Place mold in steamer with boiling water reaching 2/3 up sides of mold. Cover. Cook for 2 1/2 hours, adding water when necessary. Remove and let stand for 15 minutes before removing pudding from mold. Pudding can be stored after cooling if wrapped tightly in foil. Refrigerate. Reheat, wrapped, in 325° F. oven for 1 1/2 hours. Serve with whipped cream or hard sauce.

☆ This is really good!

apple pie

6 tart cooking apples
1 cup sugar
2 tablespoons flour
1 teaspoon cinnamon

1 teaspoon grated lemon rind
⅛ teaspoon ground cloves
⅛ teaspoon salt
Pastry for 9-inch pie shell

Peel, core, and thinly slice apples. Toss slices in a mixture of sugar, flour, and flavorings. Arrange apples in pastry shell. (make a high fluted edge). Top with a mixture of the following:

½ cup flour
¼ cup sugar
⅛ teaspoon salt

½ cup grated Cheddar cheese
¼ cup melted butter

Bake at 400°F. for about 40 minutes. Serve warm with a spoonful of sour cream on top.

☆ Note: For pastry, use one half of pastry recipe for Steak and Kidney Pie, page 41.

cheese pie
glacé

PIE

1 cup zwieback crumbs
¼ teaspoon nutmeg
¼ teaspoon cinnamon
¼ cup melted butter
12 ounces cream cheese, softened
2 eggs
½ cup sugar
½ teaspoon vanilla

Mix crumbs, nutmeg, and cinnamon together. Add butter and mix well. Press into 8-inch pie pan, bottom and sides. Blend in mixer bowl the cheese, eggs, sugar, and vanilla. Beat at high speed until very smooth and creamy. Pour into crumb crust. Bake at 350° F. for 35 minutes. Cool and top with Fruit Glacé Topping.

FRUIT GLACÉ

½ package Junket Danish Dessert
1 cup water

Combine Danish Dessert and water and cook as directed on package. Remove from heat. Fold in 1 cup drained fruit (blackberries, blueberries, Bing cherries, or peaches).

☆ Chill pie well before cutting.

apricot rum
RING

4 eggs
¾ cup oil
¾ cup apricot nectar
1 box yellow cake mix
½ cup plus 2 tablespoons
   butter
¾ cup sugar
½ cup light rum

Grease and flour a large tube pan. In a large bowl mix eggs, oil, and nectar. Add cake mix. Beat all for about 5 minutes. Pour into prepared pan. Bake at 350° F. for 50 minutes (test to be sure it's done). While cake is baking, melt butter. Add sugar and rum. When you remove cake from oven, place it on a rack and immediately pour prepared syrup slowly over cake, allowing all of syrup to sink in. Allow cake to cool for at least 1 hour before removing from the pan.

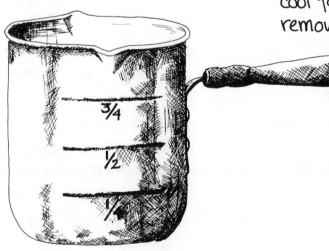

MARGARITA PIE

PIE SHELL

3/4 cup pretzel crumbs
1/3 cup melted butter
3 tablespoons sugar

Combine crumbs, butter, and sugar and press into a 9-inch, greased pie pan, bottom and sides.

FILLING

1/2 cup lemon juice
1 tablespoon unflavored gelatin
4 eggs, separated
1 cup sugar

1/4 teaspoon salt
1 teaspoon grated lemon rind
1/3 cup tequila
3 tablespoons Triple Sec

Soften gelatin in lemon juice. Beat egg yolks in top of double boiler. Blend in 1/2 cup sugar, salt, and lemon rind. Add gelatin. Cook over boiling water, stirring constantly, until slightly thickened. Transfer to a bowl and blend in tequila and Triple Sec. Chill until mixture is cold but not further thickened. Beat egg whites until foamy. Gradually beat in remaining 1/2 cup sugar until whites hold soft peaks. Slowly pour cooked gelatin mixture onto whites, folding gently but thoroughly. Let mixture stand in refrigerator until mixture mounds in a spoon. Pour into crumb shell. Chill until well set.

PRALINE COOKIES

2/3 cup margarine or butter
1 cup sugar
1/2 cup molasses
2 eggs
1/2 teaspoon vanilla
1 3/4 cups flour
1/2 teaspoon baking soda
1/4 teaspoon ground mace
1/4 teaspoon salt
1 1/2 - 2 cups coarsely chopped
    pecans

Slowly melt margarine. Cool. In mixing bowl blend melted margarine with sugar and molasses. Mix well. Add eggs and vanilla. Beat well. Sift together all dry ingredients. Beat into the molasses mixture. Add nuts. Drop by teaspoonfuls, 2 inches apart, onto greased and floured cookie sheets. Bake in preheated 375° F. oven for 8-10 minutes. Remove from pan immediately and cool on racks. Makes about 8 dozen cookies

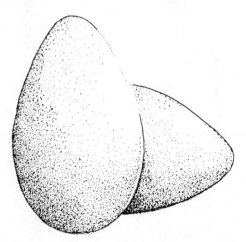

GOLDEN FRUITCAKE

1 (1 pound 12 ounce) jar maraschino cherries, drained
  well
1 (15 ounce) box golden raisins
1 cup broken walnuts
½ cup butter
1 cup sugar
4 eggs
½ teaspoon salt
1 teaspoon vanilla
2½ cups sifted flour

Snip cherries into quarters and drain on paper towels. Mix them together with raisins and nuts. Set aside. Grease and flour a large tube pan. In a large mixer bowl cream butter and sugar together until fluffy. Add eggs, beating well. Blend in 2 cups of the flour, salt, and vanilla. Beat well. Toss fruits and nuts with the remaining ½ cup of flour. Fold into batter. Pour into pan. Bake at 300°F. for 1½ hours or until cake tests done. Cool in pan for 10 minutes. Remove, cool, wrap, and chill. This fruitcake freezes well.

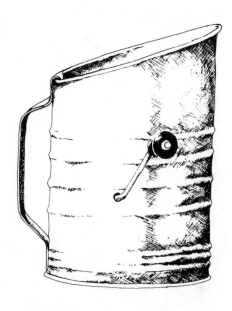

ORANGE RUM
Chiffon
Cake

2 1/4 cups sifted cake flour
1 1/2 cups sugar
3 teaspoons baking powder
1 teaspoon salt
3/4 cup fresh orange juice

1/2 cup salad oil
6 large eggs, separated
2 tablespoons grated orange rind
1/2 teaspoon cream of tartar

In medium-size mixer bowl sift together flour, sugar, baking powder, and salt. Add orange juice, oil, and egg yolks. Beat at medium speed until smooth. Add orange rind. In large mixer bowl beat egg whites and cream of tartar until stiff. Pour yolk mixture slowly over whites and fold carefully until just blended. Pour into ungreased 10-inch angel food pan. Bake at 325°F. for 65-70 minutes. Cool, inverted on rack or bottle. Remove from pan and top with:

3/4 cup orange juice
1 tablespoon lemon juice
3/4 cup sugar

1/4 cup rum
Dash of salt

Boil all ingredients together for 3-4 minutes. Slowly pour mixture over cake until it is absorbed.

pecan pie

1 8-inch unbaked pie shell
½ cup butter
½ cup sugar
⅔ cup light corn syrup
4 tablespoons maple syrup
3 eggs, slightly beaten
1 teaspoon vanilla
1 cup whole pecan halves
Dash of salt

Cream butter and sugar together thoroughly. Add syrups. Beat well. Add eggs, vanilla, and salt. Beat well. Add nuts. Pour into unbaked pie shell. (Make sure edges are crimped and high.) Bake at 325°F. for 1 hour until crust is golden. Cool thoroughly before cutting. Serve with whipped cream or ice cream topping.

super kisses

3 large egg whites
1 tablespoon vinegar
½ teaspoon salt
1 cup sugar
1 cup chopped toasted almonds
4 ounces chocolate, coarsely grated
1 (6 ounce) package chocolate bits
1 tablespoon butter
Finely chopped pistachio nuts

Beat egg whites, vinegar, and salt in a large bowl until foamy. Add sugar gradually, beating until stiff. Gently fold in almonds and grated chocolate. Drop by teaspoonfuls, at least 1 inch apart, onto greased baking sheet. Bake in 275° F. oven for 25 minutes. Cool on racks. Melt chocolate bits and butter. Swirl on tops of kisses and sprinkle with chopped pistachio nuts. Makes about 3 dozen.

peppermint fudge
SQUARES

SQUARES

½ cup flour
½ teaspoon baking powder
½ teaspoon salt
3 ounces unsweetened chocolate
⅓ cup shortening
2 eggs
1 cup sugar
1 teaspoon vanilla

Sift together flour, baking powder, and salt. Melt chocolate and shortening together over hot water. Beat eggs and add sugar and vanilla. Add chocolate and shortening. Add dry ingredients. Spread into greased 9-inch square pan. Bake at 350°F. for 20 minutes. Cool. Spread with Peppermint Frosting.

FROSTING

1 cup confectioners' sugar
Cream
¼ teaspoon peppermint extract

Combine ingredients using enough cream to make mixture spreadable. Top with chocolate sprinkles. When frosting has set cut fudge into squares. Makes 25.

☆ These peppermint fudge squares freeze well.

sponge cake

1¾ cups sifted cake flour
1 teaspoon baking powder
¼ teaspoon salt
4 eggs, separated
3 tablespoons water
1½ cups sugar
½ cup boiling water
1 teaspoon vanilla
¼ teaspoon cream of tartar
Confectioners' sugar

Beat together until light and creamy (about 10 minutes) egg yolks, 3 tablespoons water, and sugar. Add boiling water. Continue beating. Add flour, salt, and baking powder which have been sifted together. Mix well. Add vanilla. Beat egg whites and cream of tartar until stiff. Fold into yolk mixture. Pour into ungreased large tube pan. Bake at 325°F. for 55-60 minutes until cake tests done. Cool in pan on rack. Remove from pan and sprinkle with confectioners' sugar.

☆ Serve to dieting guests.

sherried apricots

1 (8 ounce) package dried apricots
Medium sherry (or use Madeira or port)

Cover apricots with water in saucepan. Bring to a boil. Drain. Place in jar (or jars). Cover with sherry or other wine. Be sure apricots are well covered. Seal jars. Let stand 2 or 3 weeks before using.

☆ Great with vanilla ice cream.

100

STRAWBERRY LIME PIE

1 tablespoon unflavored gelatin
¼ cup cold water
4 eggs, separated
1 cup sugar
⅓ cup lime juice

½ teaspoon salt
2 teaspoons grated lime rind
Green food coloring
1 cup diced fresh strawberries
1 (9-inch) baked pie shell

Soften gelatin in cold water. In top of double boiler beat egg yolks. Beat in ½ cup sugar, lime juice, and salt. Cook over hot water, stirring constantly, until thickened. Remove from heat. Add lime rind and gelatin. Stir until gelatin is dissolved. Add a few drops of green food coloring. Set aside to cool to lukewarm. Beat egg whites until stiff. Gradually beat in remaining ½ cup sugar. Fold into lime mixture. Fold in strawberries. Spoon into pie shell. (Graham cracker crust is also very good with this.) Chill until firm. Decorate with overlapping strawberry slices (and whipped cream if you're not watching calories too closely).

☆ This is a lovely, light, and refreshing pie!

PEACH
COEUR À LA CRÉME

2 tablespoons unflavored gelatin
1/3 cup cold water
1 cup light cream
6 ounces cream cheese, softened

2 cups heavy cream
1 package frozen peaches, thawed
1 cup sugar

Soften gelatin in cold water. Scald light cream. Add gelatin. Stir until blended and smooth. Cool. In mixing bowl beat cream cheese and gelatin until the mixture is light. Slowly add heavy cream, beating constantly until smooth. Add sugar. Beat well. Buzz peaches (undrained) in blender or food processor. Add to the cheese mixture. Blend well. Pour into a lightly oiled 6-cup mold (heart-shaped if you have one). Chill for several hours until set. Unmold and decorate with fresh peach slices. Serves 8-10.

sherry cream
pie

1½ cups chocolate cookie
    crumbs
¼ cup melted butter
1 tablespoon unflavored gelatin
1¼ cups cold milk
3 eggs, separated
½ cup sugar
Dash of salt
¼ teaspoon nutmeg
½ cup sherry
½ pint heavy cream, whipped

Mix cookie crumbs and butter together and press into 10-inch pie plate. Chill. Soften gelatin in ¼ cup cold milk. Put egg yolks in top of double boiler. Beat. Add sugar, salt, and remaining 1 cup milk. Stir well and cook for 10 minutes until mixture coats a spoon. Add gelatin mixture and nutmeg. Stir to dissolve. Slowly add sherry. Stir well. Chill in refrigerator until thickened. Beat egg whites until stiff. Fold into chilled custard. Fold in whipped cream. Pour into prepared pie shell. Sprinkle with grated sweet chocolate.

☆ Chill at least 4-5 hours before cutting.

SOUFFLÉ GLACÉ GRAND MARNIER

1 cup sugar
2 tablespoons water
1 tablespoon grated orange rind
6 egg yolks

½ cup Grand Marnier
2½ cups heavy cream
6 or 8 lady fingers
Cocoa

Boil water, sugar, and orange rind together for 3-4 minutes. Remove from heat. Whip egg yolks until thick. Slowly add sugar syrup, beating constantly. Beat for 10-12 minutes. Add ¼ cup Grand Marnier. Beat for 3 minutes. Whip cream until it stands in stiff peaks. Fold into other mixture. In a 1-quart soufflé dish put a layer of the mixture. Cover with a layer of lady fingers. Sprinkle lady fingers with remaining Grand Marnier. Fill dish with mixture to the top edge. Freeze. Refrigerate remaining mixture. When soufflé is frozen place a waxed paper collar, 2-3 inches high, around the dish, securing with a string. Add remaining mixture. Freeze until solid. When ready to serve remove collar. Sprinkle with cocoa.

☆ Because this freezes hard it can be safely carried to another place. It should stand out of freezer for 10 minutes before serving.

Shelburne Inn desserts

shelburne inn
cheesecake

1 cup crushed zwieback crumbs
1/4 cup melted butter
1/4 teaspoon cinnamon
1/4 teaspoon nutmeg
5 (8 ounce) packages cream
   cheese
1/3 teaspoon vanilla

1 tablespoon grated lemon rind
1 3/4 cups sugar
4 tablespoons flour
1/4 teaspoon salt
5 eggs
2 egg yolks
1/4 cup heavy cream

In a 10-inch spring-form pan, press mixture of crumbs, butter, cinnamon, and nutmeg that have been well blended. Line bottom and up sides about 1/2 inch. Set aside. Mix dry ingredients together. In a large mixer bowl put softened cream cheese, lemon rind, and vanilla. Beat until creamy. Continue beating and slowly add dry ingredients. Use rubber scraper to get all the lumps. Add eggs one at a time, beating well after each addition. Add yolks, beating thoroughly. Fold in heavy cream. Pour into prepared crust. Bake at 500°F. for 10 minutes or until golden brown. Reduce oven to 200°F. and bake for 1 hour. Cool on rack for at least 2 hours before removing pan ring. Chill. Glaze.

fruit glaze

1 pint fruit (fresh or frozen) or 1
   can of fruit, drained

1/2 package Junket Danish Dessert
1 cup water

Combine Danish Dessert and water and cook as directed on package. Remove from heat. Add fruit. Blend gently. Pour onto cheesecake. If using fresh fruit, arrange fruit on cake and spoon glaze over.
☆ Cheesecake freezes well, but do not freeze if you use the fruit.

shelburne inn chocolate cake

3 ounces unsweetened chocolate
½ cup butter
1 cup water
2 cups sifted flour
1¼ teaspoons baking soda
1 teaspoon salt
2 eggs
2 cups sugar
1 teaspoon vanilla
1 cup dairy sour cream

Melt chocolate and butter in water over low heat. Cool. Set aside. Sift together flour, baking soda, and salt. Set aside. Beat eggs, sugar, and vanilla together well. Add sour cream. Beat well. Add chocolate mixture. Beat. Add dry ingredients. Beat well. Pour into 2 8-inch pans which have been greased and floured. Bake at 350°F. for 40 minutes. Cool.

FROSTING

2 egg whites
2½ teaspoons water
½ teaspoon cream of tartar
¾ cup sugar
½ teaspoon vanilla

In top of double boiler over simmering water, beat all ingredients but vanilla until peaked. Add vanilla. Frost tops and sides of cake.

Drizzle top and sides with:
1 tablespoon butter and 1 ounce unsweetened chocolate mixed together

shelburne inn
GINGER ROLL

4 eggs
1 cup sugar
2 tablespoons orange juice
1 tablespoon orange rind
1 cup flour

1 teaspoon baking powder
1 teaspoon ginger
½ teaspoon cinnamon
¼ teaspoon salt

Line an oiled 10 x 15-inch jelly roll pan with waxed paper. Oil paper. In mixing bowl beat eggs for about 10 minutes until creamy and thick. Gradually beat in sugar. Add orange juice and rind. Combine dry ingredients and sift over egg mixture. Fold in gently. Spread into prepared pan. Bake at 375°F. for 15-17 minutes. Turn out immediately on board covered with 2 sheets overlapping waxed paper. Remove paper from cake bottom. Roll cake lengthwise in under paper. Cool. Unroll. Fill with:

 1 cup heavy cream mixed with
 ¾ cup ginger marmalade

Reroll firmly and glaze with ⅓ cup ginger marmalade that has been melted. Chill. Slice.

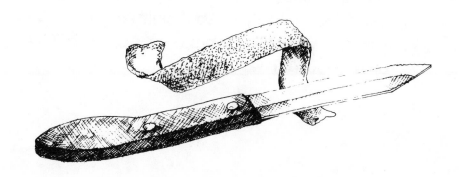

109

shelburne inn
Grasshopper pie

CRUST

1¼ cups crushed chocolate
    cookies
¼ cup melted butter

Mix together and press into a
9-inch pie pan.

FILLING

⅔ cup milk
24 large marshmallows
3 ounces green Creme de
    Menthe
1 ounce white Creme de
    Cacao
1 cup heavy cream, whipped
    stiff

Scald milk. Add marshmallows.
Stir constantly over medium
heat until all are melted. Set
aside until well cooled and
fairly stiff. Add liqueurs. Blend
well. Fold in whipped cream.
Pour into prepared shell. Freeze.
Garnish with whipped cream.
Serve right from the freezer.

☆ If you are taking this to someone's
house, don't worry about putting pie back
into the freezer. It holds. Place in freezer
when you arrive.

SHELBURNE INN
RUM TORTE

3 large packages lady fingers
1 cup rum, plus a little more
2 (3¾ ounce) packages vanilla
   pudding (Regular or Instant)
4 cups milk
1 cup heavy cream, whipped

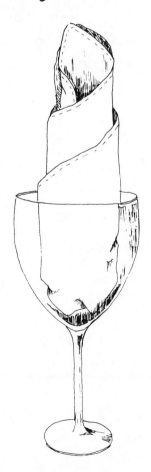

Line the bottom of a 10-inch spring-form pan with split lady fingers. Stand more fingers, side by side, against sides. Drizzle with rum. Prepare pudding mix as directed on package. (Cool if you use cooked pudding.) Pour a layer of pudding over lady fingers. Arrange more fingers on top. Add more rum, then more pudding, etc., ending with lady fingers and rum. Top with whipped cream. Chill thoroughly. Remove ring. Serve on base. You may wish to garnish the torte with some fresh strawberries or maraschino cherries.

shelburne inn
sabra pie

1¼ cups crushed gingersnaps
¼ cup melted butter
1 (3¾ ounce) package Instant
  Vanilla Pudding
1½ cups cold milk
½ cup Sabra liqueur
½ cup finely chopped
  crystalized ginger
1 cup heavy cream, whipped

Mix gingersnap crumbs and butter together. Press into 8-inch pie pan. Bake in 350°F. oven for 5 minutes. Cool. In a mixer bowl place pudding mix, milk, and Sabra. Beat as directed. Fold in ginger. Pour into prepared crust. Chill for 1 hour. Top with whipped cream. Chill.

other good things

Whether I'm a dinner guest or not, it always gives me pleasure to bring to a friend's home something I've made. I have found these recipes easy to make and sure to please.

ATLAS
E-Z
SEAL

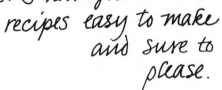

dutch tomato
RELISH

7 pounds medium-ripe tomatoes
3 pounds sugar
Vinegar
2 tablespoons whole cloves,
   tied in a bag.

Peel tomatoes and cover with vinegar. Let stand overnight. Drain well. Cut tomatoes and place in a large kettle. Add sugar and cloves. Bring to a boil, stirring to keep from catching. Simmer for a few hours, uncovered, until thick and lovely. Remove cloves. Pour into sterilized glasses. Cover with paraffin.

☆ Note: This recipe comes to me from Mrs. John Van S. Maeck.

chili sauce

50 medium-ripe tomatoes
10 medium onions
4 sweet red peppers, seeded
1 large bunch celery
1 quart cider vinegar
1 tablespoon whole allspice
1 tablespoon whole cloves
1 tablespoon whole cinnamon
3 cups sugar
2 tablespoons salt
1 nutmeg, grated

Scald, peel, and chop tomatoes. Drain. Chop remaining vegetables. Tie allspice, cloves, and cinnamon in a bag. Put all ingredients into a large kettle. Mix well. Boil for 2½ hours. Remove spice bag. Pour into sterilized jars. Seal immediately. Makes approximately 12 pints.

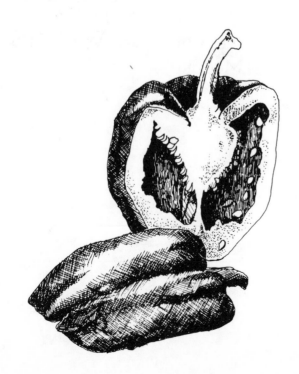

kidney bean RELISH

1 small onion, chopped
2 hard-cooked eggs, chopped
3 stalks celery, chopped
2 cups kidney beans, drained
¼ teaspoon white pepper
1 tablespoon mayonnaise
2 teaspoons mustard relish
1 teaspoon curry powder
½ teaspoon salt

Mix all ingredients together, gently and thoroughly. Refrigerate. Serve cool. Makes 6 portions.

☆ Note: This recipe comes to me courtesy of Bob Kingsley who developed it for Waybury Inn.

BREAD & BUTTER PICKLES

1 gallon medium cucumbers
8 small white onions, sliced
1 green pepper, cut into narrow strips
1 sweet red pepper, cut into narrow strips
1/2 cup salt
Cracked ice
5 cups sugar
1 1/2 teaspoons tumeric
1/2 teaspoon ground cloves
2 tablespoons mustard seed
2 teaspoons celery seed
5 cups cider vinegar

Thinly slice unpeeled cucumbers. Add onions, peppers, and salt. Cover with cracked ice. Mix thoroughly. Let stand for 3 hours. Drain. Mix together remaining ingredients. Pour over cucumber mixture. Bring to a boil. Pour into sterilized jars. Seal at once.

☆ Note: Select small narrow cucumbers (unwaxed) with small seeds

THREE FRUIT MARMALADE

Cut 1 grapefruit, 1 large orange, and 1 medium lemon into quarters. Remove seeds. Slice <u>very</u> thin. (Grate skins slightly before slicing fruit to make rinds more tender.) Measure. You must have 3½ cups. Add 3 times as much water as you have fruit. Let fruit soak in refrigerator for 24 hours. Add pinch of salt and cook until rind is tender and transparent. Measure again and add ¾ cup sugar <u>for</u> <u>each</u> cup of fruit and juice. Cook to jelly test. Add 1 cup blanched almonds. Pour into hot sterilized jars. Cover with melted paraffin. Makes 7 glasses.

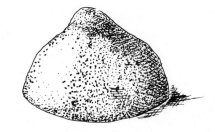

spiced pineapple

1 large pineapple
3 cups sugar
4 cups water
16 whole cloves
1 stick cinnamon
1 grated lemon rind

Remove skin, eyes, and core from pineapple. Cut fruit into strips, 2-3 inches long, ¼-½ inch thick. Boil other ingredients together until sugar is dissolved. Add fruit. Cook over medium heat until fruit is clear. Remove cinnamon stick. Pour into hot, sterilized glasses. Seal immediately.

BLUEBERRY JAM

4½ cups fresh blueberries,
    washed and picked over
Juice and grated rind of 1 lemon
7 cups sugar
1 cup liquid pectin (reserved)
Spice bag (1 cinnamon stick,
    a few cloves, piece of nut-
    meg, tied in cheesecloth)

In a large, heavy saucepan mix all ingredients but pectin. Bring to a boil, stirring. Boil for 2 minutes. Stir in pectin thoroughly. Remove from heat. Remove spice bag. Skim off foam. Stir for 5 minutes. Pour into sterilized jars. Seal with paraffin. Makes 6 glasses.

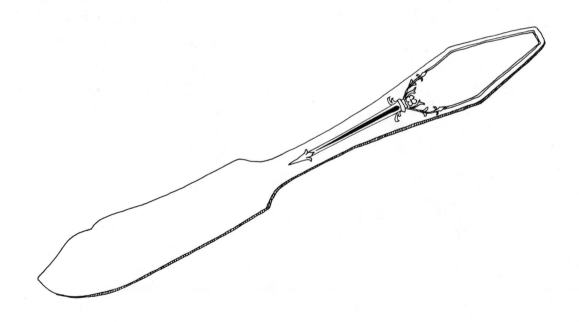

BOURBON CREAM

1 pound miniature marsh-
   mallows
24 coconut macaroons
½ cup bourbon whiskey
1 pint heavy cream

In a large bowl mix marshmallows and bourbon and
let stand, covered, for 1 hour.
Crumble the macaroons and
add to the mixture. Whip the
cream until stiff and fold into
the mixture. Put into ice trays
and freeze. It will not get
hard. Serve a spoonful top-
ped with good vanilla or coffee
ice cream and garnish with a
maraschino cherry. This mixture holds very well in the
freezer. Keep covered.

BUTTERSCOTCH RUM SAUCE

1½ cups sugar
1¼ cups light corn syrup
½ cup butter or margarine
2 cups light cream
½ teaspoon vanilla
2-3 tablespoons light rum

Cook sugar, corn syrup, butter, and 1 cup cream until it reaches 246°F. on candy thermometer or forms a hard ball when dropped into cold water. Remove from heat. Stir in remaining 1 cup of cream. Bring to a boil. Lower heat and cook, stirring until thickened, 15-20 minutes. Remove from heat. Add vanilla and rum. Cool and refrigerate. Let stand at room temperature about 1 hour before serving. Makes 3 cups sauce.

chocolate turtles

½ pound soft caramels
2 tablespoons heavy cream
1 cup pecan halves
4 squares Bakers semi-
   sweet chocolate

Melt caramels (I prefer Kraft's) in cream over hot water. Remove from heat and cool for about 10 minutes. Place nuts on waxed paper in groups of 3. Spoon caramel mixture over nuts leaving tips showing. Let stand until set (about ½ hour). Melt chocolate over hot water. Cool until lukewarm. Spread cooled chocolate over caramel. Makes about 24 turtles.